CAUTION: IMPOSTER AT WORK

CAUTION: IMPOSTER AT WORK

DARRIN SIMPSON

dsw

FOREWORD

Caution: Imposter at Work is a collection of
poems, thoughts and musings.

An invitation into my mind and heart, this project has compelled me to write more, to share more. Tangible evidence that I did more than dream, that I actually put pen to pad and created.

A labor fraught with fear that my humbug will be exposed. A labor of hubris--thinking something on these pages may be of value to you. But mostly it's a labor of hope, hope that my words, my thoughts, my efforts might bring some small bit of joy to the brave, kind soul who thought to turn its pages.

Caution

Frauds

I'm scared,

are you?

Of course you are.

Aren't we all?

I say I'm scared of spiders,

I am a bit.

But saying you are scared of spiders is easier than saying what I truly fear.

I'm afraid of you.

I'm afraid you'll discover me,

that you'll see that I'm a fraud.

Maybe that's what scares you, too?

Let's be frauds together.

I think that would be less scary.

Then maybe we can be brave, and face all the other frauds together.

Ignorance is not a virtue, fear is a vice. Beware of anyone who tells you otherwise.

Doubt thwarts your future by crippling your present.

Don't let your past define you.

Let it refine you.

Let it help shape you into the person you want to be.

If you quit, you know exactly where you end.

Where's the adventure in that?

Where you finish isn't where you start!

Keep moving!

There comes a moment when you realize

you can't waste any more time waiting!

When that moment comes, strike fast before it's gone!

Fear

I know who you are. You are an imp masquerading as a mighty monster. I know that I give you your power, or your cage. I am alert to you. I do not respect you. You do not frighten me.

You have been my constant companion. I don't remember the first time we met.

You are not my friend.

You are a fire that only burns and never warms.

You reduce me to rage and cowardice.

You have deceived me into thinking we could be a team, I should have known better.

You are a weapon that turns on its user. I'm weak when I am with you.

You are never completely defeated. You hide in the shadow, pretending to be vanquished, waiting, always waiting.

I see you plainly—twisting in your prison, the gremlin that you are. You will not control me.

I control you. I would do well to remember that.

Wake up, pour yourself a hot cup of hope, and get to it!

Liar Liar

I am a liar!
Monday is a lie!
Can't is a lie!
Blame is a lie!
Fear is a lie!
Truth is a well lit mirror in a fitting room
revealing what I already know.

What if I lived?
What if I loved?
What if I speak?
What if I write?
What if I fail!   What if I fail?   What if I fail...

What if I stopped lying?

Procrastination is a manifestation of fear.
Face the fear and get back to work.

Failure is a tremendous teacher and a terrible friend.

Your speed matters.

Your direction matters more!

The sun is a constant.

When I don't feel its rays

or see its light

it's because of where I've put myself.

Stop and Go

I persuade myself into thinking that all motion is progress.

I'm not moving forward, I'm just moving.

Stop

and think quietly.

Stop

and drink deeply.

Stop

and breathe softly.

Stop!

Be still, let it come.

Go

deliberately.

Go

incrementally.

Go

slowly, clearly

Forward.

In order to do more I have to think more.

There is a point of diminishing return

when analysis becomes paralysis.

I have to go and do,

not sit and stew.

We maximize our impact by maximizing our potential.

We maximize our potential by persistence!

Want to know how to win?

Commit to never quit! Never!

When what you want

is different than

what you get,

do you adjust?

or throw a fit?

I've spent a lot of money on things that made me feel worthless.

Enough

I am more than my bank account.

More than my GPA!

More than my likes!

More than my weight!

More than my net worth!

More than my connections!

More than what I've seen.

More than where I've been.

More than what I've read.

More than my job,

my house,

my car.

More than all of that!

I am not only more,

I am enough!

Life isn't always pleasant but that doesn't mean you can't be.

No matter where you go there you are.

You can't move fast enough to outrun yourself.

Soulmates are earned, not discovered.

Treat people with more respect than you think they deserve.

It will change both of you.

I see you

Please don't mistake *I hear you* for *I agree with you*.

I can understand you and *not* accept your ideas.

I hear you, I value you.

I want to understand you.

I respect you.

I love you.

This is my expectation for me, this is my expectation for you.

We must share our humanity.

We don't have to share an opinion.

We are a family.

We don't have to agree.

We do have to live together in peace.

I see you. I hear you. I understand you.

Do you see me?

You can do a lot of damage standing your ground

if you don't understand the ground you stand on.

Warning: when someone is trying to sell fear as an entrée, the complimentary side dishes are anger and hatred.

"I don't know" is different than "I'm not sure."

Ignorance and doubt are not synonyms.

Courage is not a cheap currency.

Getting an education is about more than money.

Lots of people have dollars but no sense.

Brilliance

Doing well on exams doesn't mean you're brilliant, it means you're proficient.

Wisdom is the application of what you have learned that benefits you and mankind.

Ego is the killer of wisdom, not ignorance.

Brilliance comes from increasing wisdom until it becomes part of your character, embedded deep in your bones.

Then you are open to bright beams of brilliance. The light from which will illuminate and chase away the darkness of ignorance and ego. It will fill your soul, it will fill the world.

When I make mountains out of minutia

I show how small my ideas are

and how big my mouth is.

I want to hear with my heart, not just my ears.

Sadly, my mouth too often gets in the way.

Sometimes it is hard to see you because I am blinded by me.

Peace comes from seeking understanding before judgment.

I would rather be understood than pitied.

The absence of malice is not the same as kindness.

Even if you have an open mind

you don't always need to have an open mouth.

Nothing in life is impossible!

Except gargling peanut butter so don't try that.

Treat praise as if it were wax wings.

Let the words lift you just be careful not to fly too close to the sun.

You don't have to be sick to get better.

Imposter

What August is Like for a Dumb Kid

August made me anxious. Not the first bit. My sister's birthday is the fourth, mine the ninth. Cake twice in a week was pretty good. Once the carnival came to town you knew the end was near. When the corn dogs were gone, so was the fun.

Even King's Department Store betrayed me—and I loved King's. You could get a salted nut roll and silly putty in the same store. The candy aisle was like a dream. But once the fair was over, it was time to buy school supplies. Those damn school supplies. They indicted me. They reminded me that I was dumb and the whole world was about to know it. Stupid Mead college-ruled notebook. How it mocked my sloppy left handed penmanship.

School meant hours of boredom and hours of hiding in plain sight. Try to look busy, try to appear engaged, try not to be noticed, try to make it to the end of the day—then you know you can go home and watch TV until bedtime.

Summer, why did you ever have to end?

It's August again, but I'm not anxious anymore. Turns out I'm not dumb. I never was. I just didn't know it.

TV

Thanks, TV, for the warm glow, the carefree hours and hours and hours. The joy of seeing happy people, beautiful people, smart people. People unlike me. Those houses! Those cars! Those adventures!

Thanks for taking care of me. For giving me something to do after school, in the evenings and on the weekend. Thanks for teaching me what to buy and what to wear.

Thanks for the test pattern on Saturday morning at 5:45 a.m. Just fifteen minutes more and then the "Super Friends!" Thanks for being my friends, Super Friends. Thanks Saturday morning for teaching me what was an important part of a well balanced breakfast.

Thanks, TV, for laugh tracks and music, the guest stars and after school specials, the game shows and variety shows, for the distraction, the reprieve, the escape. Thanks for having moms who didn't sleep after work, for dads who didn't drink too much and problems that could be resolved in thirty minutes, twenty three if you don't count commercials.

Thanks, TV, for my childhood!

Glasses

First thing on in the morning, last thing off at night, an extension of my face! "When you die, Dad, we will need to put your glasses on or people at the viewing won't know it's you," my daughter once said.

My glasses are part of my identity. A blue pair, a red pair, a green pair, clear, metal, plastic. All of the above. "How many pairs do you own?" I'm often asked. "Not enough," I reply.

They are the introduction to my face. An introduction to me. They are a reflection of how I want you to see me.

Jennifer couldn't see past my horn rimmed pair when we first met. They were not the fashion of the time. She saw a barrier to my face, a barrier to me. She eventually found my face past my glasses. She saw me. She saw my bare face, my naked face, my un-bespectacled face.

She knows my eyes. She sees me. She sees the truth. I see her. I see the truth. We see each other.

She wears contacts. I wear glasses. We still make it work.

1979 Schwinn Stingray

I am Kit, a Ty-Fighter, an X-wing starfighter or the Millennium Falcon. The power, speed and freedom of the banana seat, ape-drape handlebars, the lightning blue Schwinn Stingray!

Carol Shelby wishes he had engineered its equal. He of course, did not. Hockey stops, cops and robbers, trips to King's department store and the city's public swimming pool. My ride! A playing card in the spokes for added effect! That sound, that glorious sound! *Tickety, tickety, tickety,* faster with every pedal.

Trips to Smith's grocery store, DQ, or 7-11, no problem! With my trusty combination bike lock the world was my playground. The only kid in my neighborhood that wore a helmet had hemophilia, but the rest of us rode with our naked heads exposed. We had no idea what thrill junkies we were.

I've owned more than a dozen cars since then. Who cares! I've never traveled with more confidence or reached the level of cool I did on that bike. Not even close!

Writer's Cramp, or Swimmer's Block, or Whatever

Me: How long before you can swim after eating a sandwich?

Also Me: An hour I think? Why, are you going swimming?

Me: No, but I have writer's cramp, so I wonder if it's because I tried to write too soon after I ate.

Also me: What? That's not a thing! Writer's cramp is where your hand is tired and cramps from holding a pen or pencil for a long period.

Me: That can't be my problem. I use a keyboard.

Also me: What is cramping?

Me: My brain! I can't think of anything to write!

Also me: That's writer's block not writer's cramp! You're just being lazy and making excuses for not writing. It's a myth that inspiration is just going to "come" to you. You have to put your butt in the chair and do the work! No excuses, no distractions! Get it done! Even if it's bad writing, just write something until more ideas come. Now get to work!

Me: Must be the sandwich. I need to wait at least an hour before writing again.

Hiding

I'm hiding today because the other people are smarter.

I'm hiding today because the other people are skinnier.

I'm hiding today because my car is shabby and my clothes are too.

That's why I'm hiding today.

Why are you?

The gym in January is like the shopping mall in December. I go both places to spend my time and money trying to compensate for what I should have been doing all year.

Idahome

When I was little I didn't know how small you were.

When I was bigger, I couldn't see your majestic size.

Your unparalleled beauty and bounty.

Some view you as an oasis.

Others see you as a trap.

Both are true.

Both are lies.

We are products of our perspective more than our circumstances.

Idaho's number one export isn't potatoes, it's talent.

That's not a great slogan.

I'd stick with the potatoes.

Winter is my favorite season except for all the others.

The Van

I knew you were ours the moment I turned the key.

I couldn't afford to buy you, but I couldn't afford *not* to.

We haggled. I surrendered. You came home with me.

The kids all screamed. Jennifer smiled.

"No food in the car," we said, knowing that was a lie.

One road trip, then another.

One trip to Grandma's, one to Grandmother's, then another, then a hundred more.

You took us across the country to our new life as Hoosiers! Then you *really* got your wings.

Ten years, seven Simpsons, 259 thousand miles, 48 states, 1,000+ chicken nuggets.

So many books read aloud, so many prayers, so so so many songs.

We raised our kids in that van.

Taught three of them how to drive in it.

Showed them the Atlantic and the Pacific.

Crossed the country a half dozen times and always made it home.

Like a captain loves his ship, how I loved that van!

I Wish I Could Be Me

I wish I could be me.
I wish I could be me for at least one day.
I wish I could walk in my shoes and breathe my air.
I wish I was me.
I wish I would stop pretending to be, to live, to see.
I wish I could be me.

Seeds

"Your words are simplistic, sophomoric and weak. They lack depth of intellect and real meaning. No one will read them, they will have no value other than to demonstrate poor craftsmanship."

Be still, you feckless imp!

You have no other design than to minimize me and
all who you torment!

You do not create, you only destroy!

My words are seeds!

They will be flowers, trees, food, warmth and shelter!

They have power to provide, power to create, power to build.

You cannot belittle me!

You cannot threaten me!

I will give the world my words.

I will scatter them to the wind

and wait patiently for them to bloom.

I Am Two Men

I am two men.

The one I hope to be

and the one I am.

One gives me hope.

One gives me pause.

Everyday I wrestle to see who will come out on top.

I am grateful for those who have been kind to me.

I am also grateful for those who have been truthful.

I'm especially grateful for those who have been both.

City Boy, Country Girl

Jennifer grew up swimming in a ditch. I went to the city pool. She rode her bike six miles to go to Lloyd's Country Store. I walked to King's, Smith's grocery store, 7-11, Dairy Queen and Taco Time.

I had cable 29 channels, 29! She had rabbit ears, four channels, and only channel 8 came in good. I was a city kid from Burley: population 8,000. She was a country girl from Sunnydell: population a few hundred, give or take. We still made it work.

Now, we live in a neighborhood that has 17,000 people per square mile, 100+ restaurants, three movie theaters, three grocery stores, and roughly 12,000 dry cleaners... all within walking distance of our *spacious* 1100 square foot apartment with 250 channels, 250! We're still making it work.

I Was Here

I was here!

Did you see me?

Did you hear me?

Did you know?

Did you care?

Was I noticed?

Was I important?

I WAS HERE!

Did I see you?

Did I hear you?

Did I know you?

Did I care for you?

Did I notice you?

You are so important!

I KNOW YOU ARE HERE!

Maybe It's Bacon?

As kids, we'd wake up in the morning to the smell of bacon followed by two immediate reactions:

Reaction One: Yes! Bacon!

Reaction Two: You know mom only makes bacon about twice a year. Then she uses the bacon grease for the rest of the year to grill pancakes.

Life is filled with those "maybe it's bacon" moments. The secret is not to be sad there's no bacon but to be happy that there are pancakes.

A donut is a bagel that just didn't stop believin'.

There is nothing much better than the feeling of sleeping until you want to wake up.

Why do we tell ourselves that if we share what we produce with the world it must be brilliant or it's humbug?

That we are either masters or charlatans?

Where is the space for authenticity and growth in that?

When we are brave enough to stand on stage, we show we are doers, not just dreamers.

I want to die like a warrior, armor clad and filled with honor.

I don't want to die day by day.

The slow corrosive death of a coward

one who refused to dream, to fight, to live!

What if the story you've been telling yourself your whole life isn't true?

What if you're not the hero?

What if you are the dragon?

Then what?

Today's The Day!

Today's the day I win!

Today's the day I surrender.

Today's the day I make new friends!

Today's the day I am vanquished.

Today's the day I start over!

Today's the day I quit.

Today! Today. Today?

Maybe it'd be better to wait and see how tomorrow looks?

Knots

Knots.

I'm no good at tying them.

I can't make the rope do what I'd have it do.

"See, look here, it's easy,"

someone would say before they showed me the correct way to tie the thing.

It was no help. I just couldn't learn to tie those things.

I was eight before I could tie my own shoes and nearly thirteen before I could tie a necktie.

Bow ties and square knots, half high, boom hitch, no thanks.

It's all a mess to me.

I guess I'm better at untying them.

Like the constant knot I had in my stomach as a child.

That aching, nagging, haunting knot that never left me and always stayed, contorted, tangled and twisted in my gut.

It brought me guilt, worry and shame.

I don't know exactly what kind of knot it was, but I'm sure glad I figured how to untie it.

Maybe that's why I just leave knots alone.

Airplanes

At a thousand feet you can see the wonder of man.

All those lights, thousands of them!

Each one represents a home, a family, a life!

Filled with all the complexities of humans.

At forty thousand feet you see the wonders of God, stars!

Millions and millions of them!

Each a testament to His magnitude and majesty, with all the wonder and glory!

You Are Wrong!

You are wrong!

I'm sure of it!

You need to think more clearly!

You need to change your mind!

You need to be more open minded!

You need to think about things more deeply!

YOU NEED TO LISTEN MORE AND SHOUT LESS!

You need to be more like me, because I am right!

At least I think I am.

I feel like I am.

I thought I was.

Either way, you're still wrong and that's what matters.

I often embarrass myself when I display my lack of knowledge and my overabundance of passion at the same time.

It's a wondrous thing to ponder, the power of a baby. Here they are, helpless, and yet they hold us captive. All who have held and loved a child have marveled and trembled at the thought of the awesome responsibility now placed in their arms. How could such a tiny person bring so much fear, sobriety, wonder and love? So much love!

The clouds didn't lose their magic, you just forgot to believe.

One of the simplest and most profound lessons

I have ever learned in my life is this:

No matter where I go, there I am!

Derivative

All the poems have been written.

Playwrights, authors, artists all need to close up shop.

All that's left is derivative!

All the flowers have bloomed.

All the birds have sung.

No more sunsets required.

No more beach walks needed.

Babies can stop laughing.

Lovers can stop kissing.

We've seen it all!

Unless it's your baby, your beach,

your garden, your page, your kiss.

Then drink it! Sing it! Live it! Experience it anew!

Write it, draw it, tell it, show if you can.

Capture in some way the essence of life

with its relentless repetition and unique expression.

At Work

Second Chances

I believe in second chances.

I am a product of them.

Second chances at life.

Second chances at love.

Second chances at friendship.

So many second chances.

I've been given second chances,

I've given them in return.

To forgive is a gift,

to be forgiven is a joy unparalleled.

I believe in second chances.

Second chances are grace,

a spark of the divine, a light in the dark,

a beacon, a life line.

I will give second chances.

I will extend grace.

I believe in second chances.

My Bookstore

My bookstore smells like coffee, I bet yours does too.

Most bookstores sell coffee now.

My bookstore sells all the newest titles

and many of the old faves too.

My book store features local authors and highlights their work.

I hope yours does too.

My local bookstore's books cost a bit more

than if I buy them online.

I buy them there anyway.

I hope you do, too.

I Love Airports, I Hate Airports

I love airports. They bring the people I love to me!

Those people come from far away

and in a few hours they are back in my arms!

I love airports. They mean I am going somewhere!

Off to adventure! To see, explore, reunite!

I hate airports. They are where I say goodbye.

Those people I love leave my arms and go off

on some tin can in the sky and zoom away from me.

I hate airports. They remind me that the adventure is over.

All that's left is memory.

Thanks airports for bringing us together!

Thanks airports for taking me to family and friends!

Shame on you airports! Think about what you have done!

How do you live with yourself?

It's Her Bed

I will never make my wife's bed exactly right. I know what you're thinking. "You said, 'My wife's bed,' actually the bed belongs to both of you." I guess that is true in theory. However, in practice, not a chance.

We both know she is completely in charge of the bed. How many throw pillows, where they all go, when we use a duvet, when we don't. When we change the sheets, when we need all new bedding, and definitely, exactly, how the bed should be made. Her dominance over the bed is made most apparent at night when she occupies 80% of it.

Sure she "includes" me in the decision making process. Much like you might alert the monarch that Parliament is dissolving. Or more like the king in chess: the game is not over until he is defeated, but we all know he has limited ability, and is frankly useless. The bed is her domain, she is the sovereign. I'm okay with it because I've slept alone and I don't recommend it.

Let Your Light Shine

Let's talk a little truth.

Someone plays the piano better than you. Play anyway!

Someone paints better than you. Paint anyway!

Someone writes better than you. Write anyway!

Jesus did not say you should only remove your light from under the bushel if it's a 100 watt bulb! He wants that little light to shine no matter who you think is shining brighter! We need your light!

So, write that essay, sing that song, paint that painting,

knit that scarf, do the things!

Trust me, you'll be glad you did!

When I fill my head with hate I empty my heart of love.

You Can Do Anything

When You Get Home From Work

Home from work and off to space!

Or a submarine adventure!

There may even be a castle to storm or an evil wizard to vanquish.

No doubt there will be dance shows and plays to produce.

If we are lucky, there might even be an Olympic medal or two!

The kids are so little but their imaginations are so big!

You can be and do anything when you get home from work!

The Universe and Me

The universe is very big.

I am very small.

I am part of the universe.

I am part of something big.

I see the stars.

Do they see me?

The light I see takes years to get to me. Years.

The stars are billions of years old. Billions.

The stars I see shining are from trillions of miles away. Trillions.

Trillions and billions and years and years.

Trillions and billions and years and years!

I am part of something special!

I am part of something big!

I am part of years and years!

Billions and billions!

Trillions and trillions!

I am small. I am important. I can shine.

Home

Home is where you know who you are.

No need to compare yourself

but the confidence to complete yourself.

Where you are safe and motivated.

Where there is rest and energy.

Stability and mobility.

Home is where conflict gives way to love.

Where the best version of yourself is allowed full expression

especially in the early stage.

Home is where you sing out loud,

cry hard

and sleep deep.

Home is where we are forgiven and give forgiveness.

Home is where we are bound by love,

moved by love, cradled by love,

learn to let go,

and discover who we are.

To be the person you want to be, you must enable others to be the person they want to be.

Fear is the doorway to defeat, courage is the doorway to victory!

Boston = Freedom

Freedom is this city's story. A narrative nearly 400 years old. "We came here to be free of the Church of England," "Down with King George!" and all of that. Pilgrims and patriots and so many other tired and poor souls yearning to be free.

Of course that story is too simple. Over the centuries, so much suffering and pain has been inflicted upon those who were not privileged enough to be celebrated but were every bit as much the pilgrim and the patriot.

For me, this city has been freedom. Freedom to be me. Here, I feel safe. Safe enough to say how I vote, safe enough to say how I feel, safe enough to think out loud and be heard, not questioned, or frowned upon, or ridiculed. Freedom to think deeply, freedom to assemble with those who also want to think, to dream, to be.

You're a tough old town and freedom is in your bones. I feel it calling to me. I feel it like a beacon, see it like a lamp in the dark, calling me to be free.

Exclamations and Questions

I want them to put country over party!

What am I doing to heal the partisan divide?

I'm sick and tired of their outrage!

What am I doing to bring about peace?

They are the problem!

How am I contributing to the solution?

They hate America!

What will I do to show my love of country?

Their motives are corrupt!

How do I ensure my motives are pure?

Shout them down!

How will I listen more?

I hate them!

Am I brave enough to love everyone?

Bravery isn't a character trait, it's a recipe.

1 part Courage

1 part Vision

2 parts Faith

Blend together and bake with adversity.

If you don't understand someone

after walking a mile in their shoes,

walk another mile.

Joy is not a zero sum game.

Our choices reveal our character more than our abilities do.

Friends don't judge you for your scars

they relate to you because of them.

My burdens got much lighter when I helped carry yours.

I'm Listening

I heard the birds but never listened.

I was over forty before I knew how distinct they were.

I was staying alone at a hotel in West Virginia.

The front desk was advertising a bird walk for the next morning.

So I went on a bird walk with Bob the naturalist.

Bob identified all kinds of birds just by listening.

How had I missed them?

They are loud, persistent and unique.

I must have trained my ear not to hear.

Taught myself to tune them out.

What else have I learned not to listen to?

What else have I taught myself to not see.

What beautiful, singular voices am I missing?

What colors and sounds escape me?

What do I let blend into the background noise?

Do I hear you? Do I see you? Are you singing to me?

Please forgive me. I'm trying to learn.

I'm trying to hear. I'm trying to see. I'm listening.

When I see someone change for the better,

I want to be the kind of person to say,

"I knew you could!"

not

"Who would've thought?"

Instead of treating people in kind, just be kind.

How different would life be if we viewed the people around us not as our competition but our teammates?

One of the greatest challenges and joys in life comes from learning how to sincerely celebrate other's accomplishments.

Live your life

with the confidence of Superman

and the humility of Clark Kent.

Love is power. The more we have, the more unstoppable we are.

If you want to have meaning in your life,

plant trees whose shade you will never sit under.

ABOUT THE AUTHOR

Darrin Simpson lives in Cambridge, Massachusetts. He enjoys walking to Spy Pond, kayaking, cheering for the Red Sox and the Celtics, and hanging out with his amazing family.

You can learn more about Darrin and his writing projects by visiting darrinsimpsonwrites.com